LOVE

# POTiOns
## & *charms*

Over 50 ways to seduce, bewitch, and cherish your lover

*Francis Melville*

**BARRON'S**

A QUARTO BOOK

Copyright © 2001 Quarto Inc.

First edition for the United States, its
territories and dependencies and
Canada published in 2001 by
Barron's Educational Series, Inc.

All inquiries should be addressed to:
Barron's Educational Series, Inc.
250 Wireless Boulevard
Hauppauge, NY 11788
http://www.barronseduc.com

ISBN 0-7641-5364-1
Library of Congress Catalog Card No.
00-104-543

QUAR.LOPO

Conceived, designed and produced by
Quarto Publishing plc
The Old Brewery
6 Blundell Street
London N7 9BH

**Editor**  Steffanie Diamond Brown
**Art editor/designer**  Julie Francis
**Copy editor**  Claire Waite
**Photographer**  Will White
**Stylist**  Lindsay Phillips
**Illustrator**  Elsa Godfrey
**Proofreader**  Neil Cole
**Indexer**  Dorothy Frame

**Art Director**  Moira Clinch
**Publisher**  Piers Spence

Manufactured by Regent Publishing
Services Ltd., Hong Kong
Printed by Midas
Printing Ltd., China
9 8 7 6 5 4 3 2 1

# CONTENTS

NOTE
The author, publisher, and copyright holder have made
every reasonable effort to ensure that the recipes and
formulas in this book are safe when used as instructed, but
assume no responsibility for any injury or damage caused or
sustained while using them. This book is not intended as a
substitute for the advice of a health care professional.

# Introduction

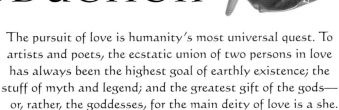

The pursuit of love is humanity's most universal quest. To artists and poets, the ecstatic union of two persons in love has always been the highest goal of earthly existence; the stuff of myth and legend; and the greatest gift of the gods— or, rather, the goddesses, for the main deity of love is a she.

## The goddess of love

The Greeks called her Aphrodite; to the Romans, she was known as Venus. She is the goddess of every aspect of love between humans, from the most carnal to the most tender. She celebrates the pleasures of sex and teaches the principles of making love as a sacred act requiring the full-hearted conjoining of masculine and feminine energies.

## Connecting to the goddess

As the highest celebration of the gift of life, making love is what we are here to do. To achieve the heights of lovemaking, we need to be in fine condition in body, heart, and soul. If we have an impaired function or a lack of desire, then a remedy must be found. Such remedies are named after the goddess herself: aphrodisiacs. These are the special foods, plants, and potions that reconnect us to the goddess. Perhaps the most basic aphrodisiac is water: it was from the sea that Aphrodite rose. Her name means "of the foam," and is celebrated by Homer, who wrote:

*...the most magnificent, most charming goddess escaped from the foam.*
*Fragrant herbs shot forth from under her flying feet.*
*This garlanded one who slipped from the foam,*
*Gods and humans, they named her Aphrodite,*
*She who was nourished by the foam.*

## The life source

Water is the source of all things, the vital fluid of life. Drinking sufficient water is the first rule of good health, followed by good nutrition. The simplest aphrodisiacs are those foods that are sacred to Venus/Aphrodite: the fruits of the sea, and many of the most delicious vegetables and fruits of the land. Eating these foods on a daily basis is the key to staying fit for love.

## Magical herbs

To fine-tune our physical prowess, we can turn to those "fragrant herbs" that Homer suggests were born with the goddess. The use of these herbs is recorded in the very earliest writings. The sacred soma of the ancient Indian Vedic texts is celebrated in the following hymn:

*We have drunk the Soma*
*We have become immortal*
*We have gone to the light*
*We have found the gods.*
    The Rig-Veda

We know that the soma is some sort of plant; the ancient texts even tell us how to prepare the potions that forged ecstatic union with the gods. Sadly, however, we have long forgotten which plant it was. It is also possible that the plant no longer exists. Indeed, some aphrodisiacs were so prized that they were picked to extinction. One example is satyrion, the

aphrodisiac referred to by ancient Greek and Roman poets. In his novel *Satyricon*, Petronius wrote:

*We saw in the chambers persons of both sexes, acting in such a
way that I concluded
they must all have been drinking satyrion.*

## Healthful herbs

Aphrodisiacs work in many different ways. Some look after vital metabolic processes; some are tonics, supporting certain organs to sustain vitality; others affect the reproductive system, promoting fertility and the healthy functioning of our sex organs; and some work subtly on our senses, soothing and transporting through scent or delighting our taste buds. The most highly prized and elite group of aphrodisiacs has a direct action on the libido, and can actually provoke desire and improve performance.

## A journey of discovery

The development of an interest in aphrodisiacs can be a fascinating journey of discovery, leading to the most intimate center of our beings. It is an initiation into the very heart of our desires. Not only is it important to learn which plants and foods have aphrodisiac qualities, we must also discover which ones suit us best, given our individual needs, tastes, and desires.

## Revelation and rediscovery

Upon reading this book, you will be surprised to discover how many of your favorite flowers, spices, essential oils, foods, and herbs have long been cherished for their aphrodisiac qualities. Learning how to use these natural gifts to enhance your sensuality will arouse your creative instincts and help you achieve sensual and spiritual fulfillment. Always remember that the greatest aphrodisiac is you: your imagination, appreciation, and capacity to love. It is your presence that brings these potions and charms to life.

## Some words of advice

In the words of the great physician and alchemist Paracelsus "Everything is poison. Nothing is poison." Almost anything can be bad for us if we take too much of it. Some of the substances referred to in this book can cause damage to health if taken in excess over prolonged periods of time, and may not mix well with alcohol or drugs—prescribed or otherwise. Indications are provided in the text where caution is necessary. Use your judgment, and consult a doctor if in doubt.

When using the recipes in this book, make sure your utensils and hands are washed using fresh water. Where unfamiliar ingredients are mentioned, consult the Directory (page 122) for more information. Use the Buyers' Guide (page 126) to locate suppliers.

*chapter one*

# TEMPLE OF
## ⊙ OF

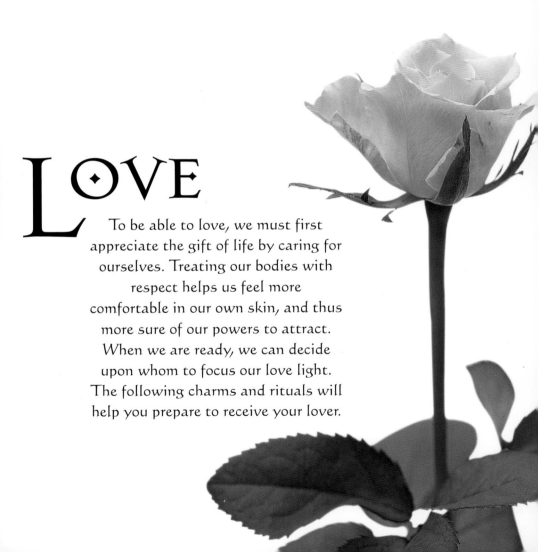

# LOVE

To be able to love, we must first appreciate the gift of life by caring for ourselves. Treating our bodies with respect helps us feel more comfortable in our own skin, and thus more sure of our powers to attract. When we are ready, we can decide upon whom to focus our love light. The following charms and rituals will help you prepare to receive your lover.

# HEARTSEASE CHARM

*Sprinkle on the eyelids of your
coveted love and they will be yours*

## YOU WILL NEED

*flowering heartsease*

*grapeseed or
sunflower oil*

*mortar and pestle*

*glass jar*

*sterilized bottle*

Heartsease, the wild pansy, has always been associated with love. According to legend, the flower was originally white. When struck by one of Cupid's bolts, it was tinged purple by the wound, hence the common name "love-lies-bleeding."

The use of heartsease as a love charm is celebrated by William Shakespeare in *A Midsummer Night's Dream*, when Oberon, the Fairy King, decides that he needs its power:

*Yet marked I where the bolt of Cupid fell
It fell upon a little western flower.
Before, milk-white; now, purple with love's wound;
The maidens call it love-in-idleness.
Fetch me that flower; the herb I shew'd thee once;
The juice of it on sleeping eyelids laid,
Will make man or woman madly dote,
Upon the next live creature that it sees.*

To use heartsease in this manner might take some careful arranging, but should you get the opportunity, here's how to be sure that you have some heartsease juice at hand.

## METHOD

Pick some flowering heartsease on a sunny day. Pound it into a mortar, then add some grapeseed or sunflower oil. Pour the mixture into a jar. Leave in a warm place for two weeks, then strain into a sterilized bottle. Preserve for one year.

# THE
# BAY LEAF DREAM

*To inspire dreams of
your destined lover*

## YOU WILL NEED

*bay leaves*

*pins*

The art of divination—the attempt to read the future—has been a matter of great interest to all cultures in all times, particularly in the ancient world. People like the Celts and the Native Americans believed that nature was their personal guide, and that by employing certain herbs or stones in a ritual way, they could tap into their spirits and be guided by them through visions or dreams. One plant that has been used in this way for thousands of years in Europe is sweet bay, or the bay laurel, most commonly known to us as the bay leaf used in cooking. The bay leaf has excitant and narcotic qualities, and was formerly used to treat hysteria. Bay leaf is still used to inspire dreams of the person with whom one is destined to fall in love. Here is a traditional European ritual for St. Valentine's Eve, to inspire a visionary dream of the true object of one's desire.

## METHOD

Make a tea from bay leaves and pour it into a warm bath at night. Relax in it for ten minutes, tuning into your heart and your love. Calmly emerge from the bath and put on freshly washed nightclothes. Pin a bay leaf to each corner of your pillow, and place a fifth leaf underneath it. Climb into a freshly made bed and repeat the following rhyme before falling asleep:

*Good Valentine, be kind to me
In dreams let me my true love see.*

# VERVAIN FIRE CHARM

*Call on the elements to ignite your lover's passion*

## YOU WILL NEED

*dried vervain*

*brown paper*

*ink pen*

*fire*

Using fire to seal written spells or wishes is standard magical practice in many parts of the world. The idea is that spells are more powerful if written as well as recited, and the burning of a written spell will seal its intent, while the smoke bears the wish into the spiritual realm. To make a powerful wish regarding a matter of love, first take a vervain bath (see Sweet Dream Bath, page 18). While relaxing in the warm water, consider the nature of your wish carefully.

## METHOD

Take an ink pen (representing the element of water) and inscribe upon brown paper (representing the element of earth) your wish (representing the element of air), speaking the words out loud as you write. Take a sprig of dried vervain and wrap it in the paper.

The vervain will act as a mediator on behalf of its mistress, Venus. Prepare a fire and, when aflame, turn toward the east and say "Hail to the east and the spirits of air." Recite your wish, then say "So mote it be." Now turn to the south and say "Hail to the south and the spirits of fire" and repeat the process; turn to the west and say "Hail to the west and the spirits of water" and repeat the process once again. Finally, turn to the north and say "Hail to the north and the spirits of earth" and repeat the process one last time. Carefully place your wish in the fire while silently repeating it. Watch the transforming flames consume your wish while the smoke carries it heavenward, and thank the four directions and elements in turn for their assistance.

# Sweet Dream Bath

*Prepare your body and soul to dream of love*

## You will need

*dried vervain*

*muslin bag*

A long soak in a warm bath is the perfect way to unwind, clearing the mind and purifying the body. A traditional bath additive was vervain, a delicate, unassuming wildflower native to Europe. Ruled by Venus, vervain was also considered an aphrodisiac, and was commonly used in love potions. Magicians believed that it strengthened their spells, and country folk used it to help them have pleasant dreams that would come true. Medicinally, vervain relieves insomnia and soothes the nerves, while relaxing both mind and body. All of these qualities add up to a very special potion that can help inspire true love dreams. The following ritual is best performed on a Friday, the day of Venus.

## Method

Take a handful of dried vervain and place it in a muslin bag. Tie the bag onto the hot tap of your bath, so that the water can flow through it. Run a deep bath, turn off the ringer on your telephone, and lie back and relax. Starting with your toes, consciously relax every part of your body. Empty your mind and allow the vervain to penetrate your entire being. With the sacred herb's protection, you can feel completely at ease. Gently cleanse yourself in preparation to receive a gift of vision from Venus, goddess of love. Dry yourself slowly and carefully, then don your favorite bedclothes and get into a warm bed. Give yourself plenty of time to fall asleep, counting your blessings as you drift off. Who knows what will be revealed unto you?

# BED OF ROSES

*A ritual to forge a*
*union of true love*

## YOU WILL NEED

*red rose*

*white rose*

*gold ring*

*silver ring*

*copper ring*

The rose is the very symbol of love, its different colors denoting different nuances of the emotion: white for pure, virginal, or platonic love, and red for passionate, amorous love. The rose is associated as well with wine, sensuality, and seduction. As the emblem of Venus and Aphrodite, it represents love, life, creation, fertility, and beauty. Roman newlyweds were crowned with rose garlands, as were statues of Venus, Cupid, and Bacchus. Together, the red and the white rose symbolize the union of opposites. In alchemy, they represent the marriage of fire and water, the union of the masculine and feminine principles. Here is a simple ritual to magically forge a union between a man and a woman.

## METHOD

Take a red and a white rose, the buds of which are just beginning to open. Hold the stems together and slide a gold ring over them (gold is the metal of the sun, the masculine principle). Next, slide on a silver ring (silver is the metal of the moon, the feminine principle), and then slide on a copper ring (copper is the metal of Venus—the planet as well as the goddess—who will assist the union of the couple). Now place the "wedded" roses on the pillow of a freshly made bed. Say a prayer or make a wish that the couple represented by the roses should come together. If the roses are still fresh and blooming in the morning, you may take this as a good sign.

# THE
# YARROW DREAM

*A spell to help you conjure
a vision of your dream lover*

## YOU WILL NEED

*flowering yarrow*

*cloth*

*needle and thread*

Yarrow has been used by many different civilizations throughout history. The ancient Chinese cast yarrow stalks to "read the runes" when consulting the *I Ching*, their book of divination, a practice that continues today. That the culture of Anglo-Saxon England used the herb in the same way is one of those tantalizing mysteries of humans and nature. The obvious answer is that the herb wasn't chosen randomly, and that it really does have these apparently magical properties. In parts of England, young women would tickle the inside of their noses with a feathery yarrow leaf, hoping their nose would bleed as they recited this rhyme:

*Yarroway, yarroway, bears a white blow,
If my true love loves me, my nose will bleed now.*

Here is a traditional recipe for identifying your dream lover.

## METHOD

Pick a handful of flowering yarrow on a Friday morning when the dew has dried, and sew it up in a pouch. Place the pouch under your pillow and say these words before going to sleep:

*Thou pretty herb of Venus' tree thy true name it is yarrow;
Now who my bosom friend must be pray tell thou me tomorrow.*

When you wake, you should know your destined love.

# CLOAK AND SLIPPERS

*A balm to soothe and comfort
the grace of womanhood*

## YOU WILL NEED

2 oz (60g) lady's
mantle

1 pint (½L) brandy
or vodka

2 oz (60g) lady's
slipper

mortar and pestle
glass jar
glass bottle

Many plants have been named for the Virgin Mary; most include the prefix "lady's." One such plant is lady's mantle, often referred to as "a woman's best friend" due to its abundance of medicinal qualities serving women's health. Lady's mantle is ruled by Venus, goddess of love. This attractive plant was named after the shape of its leaves, which resemble the folds of the Virgin Mary's cloak, as depicted in Renaissance paintings. Lady's mantle is an excellent gynecological herb. It is used to tone the reproductive system, to help ease period pain, and to assist in the transition of menopause. It works well in combination with lady's slipper, which is used to relieve anxiety. Lady's slipper is ruled by Sirius, the star closely connected with Isis, the Egyptian mother goddess. The combination of the two plants soothes and comforts the grace of womanhood.

## METHOD

Pick some lady's mantle and some lady's slipper on a sunny Friday morning during the waxing moon, when the plants are just beginning to bloom. Dry them in the shade. On a following Friday, grind the plants to a powder. Place the powders in a glass jar, mixing them together, and cover with brandy or vodka. Seal, then place in a warm, dark spot for two weeks. Strain the potion into a glass bottle. Take 1 tsp (5ml) three times a day to ease period pains or menopause symptoms, and to soothe the nerves.

# Queen's Delight

*A wonderfully healing lotion for
a fresh, beautiful complexion*

## You will need

*1 oz (30g) fresh
queen's delight root*

*1 cup (250ml) water*

*½ oz (15g) cocoa
butter*

*3 tbsp (45ml)
wheatgerm oil*

*2 tbsp (30ml)
evening primrose oil*

*2 tsp (10ml) beeswax*

*1 tsp (5ml) clear
honey*

*essential oils of
frankincense and
myrrh*

*rose, ylang ylang, or
jasmine perfume oil*

*dark glass bottle*

The queen's delight plant grows in the southern United States, and was brought to Europe by early visitors to the New World. It was given its name because of its wonderful ability to cure a wide variety of skin conditions. The heavy lead-based make-up that was so fashionable in the 18th century wreaked havoc with ladies' complexions, and queen's delight proved an indispensable ally in helping them keep their looks and health. It is the root that is used, and it is generally thought to work best when fresh. Here is a special recipe for a curative and rejuvenating body lotion.

## Method

Finely slice the queen's delight root and boil it gently for ten minutes in water. Strain out the root and reduce the liquid. Set aside to cool. Put the cocoa butter, wheatgerm oil, and evening primrose oil in a bowl. Fill a pan with fresh water, then heat the water and dissolve the beeswax and honey in it. Whisk in the queen's delight water, one spoonful at a time. Add five drops each of frankincense and myrrh essential oils and five drops of either rose, ylang ylang, or jasmine perfume oil to the potion. Mix well, then store in a dark glass bottle. The potion can be kept in the refrigerator for up to a month.

# THE OUTER TEMPLE

*Cleanse and purify the
outer temple of your love*

## You will need

*sage, cut into 6 in
(150mm) lengths*

*length of red wool*

The outer temple of your love is your home. Your home is your sacred outer space, and as such, it should be as positive and as life enhancing as possible. Energy must be allowed to flow unhindered, so it is necessary do away with clutter and the dust of days gone by. Possessions you no longer need or appreciate should be removed, but pause to honor the things you love, and be thankful for all the things that allow you to live in comfort. Once you have tidied up, you can cleanse and purify the energy of your outer temple. On a breezy day, light a smudge stick and let the purifying smoke fill every corner of your home. Imagine it neutralizing stagnant energy and chasing out sneaky spirits. When the entire house is fumigated, throw open the doors and windows, filling your home with the air of new promise. Breathe in the fresh air and feel the change of energy. Here's how to make your own smudge stick.

## Method

Pick some sage just before it blooms, and hang it in a warm place to dry. Bind the dried herbs together with red wool. Red is the color of the south, and the element of purifying fire. Wind the wool from the bottom of the bound herbs to an inch or two from the top, and back down again. To use your smudge stick, light the end of it, then blow out the flame. The stick will smolder and release its perfumed smoke. Use it like a magic cleansing wand.

# True Love Knot

*A ritual to divine
your future lover*

## You will need

*herb paris*

*white linen
handkerchief*

*matches or a
cigarette lighter*

Herb Paris is an unusual plant found growing in northern Europe. Its leaves appear in the shape of a love knot, hence its country names "true love knot" and "true love." Its seeds and berries are narcotic, having a somewhat similar effect to opium. In large doses, the herb is poisonous, but in safe amounts it was once considered an antidote for the plague. Given its toxicity, it is not recommended for use as a love potion, but here is a ritual in which it is used as a divinatory love charm.

## Method

Sit silently in a room from midnight until one o'clock in the morning, either with another person or by yourself. During this hour, pull out a hair from your head for each year of your age and lay them on a white linen handkerchief. Place a stem of herb Paris on the handkerchief as well. When the hour has passed, burn each of your pulled-out hairs separately, while reciting:

*I offer this my sacrifice,
To him (or her) most precious in my eyes
I charge thee now come forth to me,
That I this minute may thee see.*

Your future partner should appear in the room after your last hair has been burned. If there is another person with you, you should not be able to see their vision, nor they yours.

# THE
# ALTAR OF LOVE

*A sensuous gift for your
body, the altar of your love*

## YOU WILL NEED

*olive oil*

*essential oils of
frankincense and
myrrh*

Our body is our greatest friend and ally, housing our heart, spirit, and soul. The ancients believed that we are a microcosm, a reflection of the entire universe. This is what is meant by the idea that we are made in the likeness of God. All life is in us. We may look in the mirror at times and be dissatisfied with what we see, but the fact is that we are what we are. In order to feel good about ourselves, it can help to remember just how fortunate we are. Our love starts with our joy at being alive, our grateful acknowledgment of our amazing sensory selves. Here is a simple, effective way to revitalize respect for your body, the altar of your love.

## METHOD

To appreciate something is to value it highly, be thankful for it, understand it, and take full account of it. We can apply the appreciation process to reappraise ourselves. Each of our wondrous senses is an incredible gift, as is each finger, toe, and limb. With some golden olive oil perfumed with a few drops of frankincense and myrrh, we can reanoint ourselves as our own chosen ones. Apply this potion to your entire body, from head to toe, honoring and acknowledging each body part. By the time you have finished, you will have a new resolve to treat yourself well. Most important of all, you will have an intimate rapport with your brand new best friend: you.

# THE
# INNER SANCTUM

*Seduce and entice your lover in
your own sensuous inner sanctum*

## YOU WILL NEED

*essential oils of
neroli, rose absolute,
jasmine absolute,
sandalwood, ylang
ylang*

*incense burner*

Your bedroom is your love chamber. This is where you receive your lover, and invite him or her to share your most intimate pleasures. The whole room should thus express the shades of your love and the tones of your desire. The art of seduction involves combining the perfect textures of light, warmth, and smell to create the right feeling. Rich, dark colors and soft, heavy fabrics create a sultry atmosphere. Fresh flowers can add beauty and life. Ornaments can be tactile, symbolic, simple, or sophisticated. Nothing says "let's make love" better than a large, comfortable, solid bed with delicious sheets and covers. If you don't have a comfortable bed, a futon or mattress covered in satin or velvet, or soft, comfortable cushions will do just fine. And don't forget the floor: a soft, luxurious floor covering can add an extra dimension to your erotic options. The air in the room should be fresh, but subtly scented. To create a soft, sensual fragrance, try this amorous blend of essential oils.

## METHOD

Combine two drops of neroli, three drops each of rose absolute, jasmine absolute, and sandalwood with four drops of ylang ylang. Add some water to this mixture and place in an incense burner. The scents will blend and disperse, spreading an air of seduction throughout the room.

The strongest temple

# LOVES ME, LOVES

In European folklore, numerous plants and flowers were used as helpers and oracles in the art of love. We are all familiar with "kissing under the mistletoe," which originated as an opportunity for young men to publicly express their affection for a certain girl without causing a scandal. To this day, most children are familiar with the daisy game, where petals are picked off one by one while reciting alternately "She (he) loves me, she (he) loves me not."

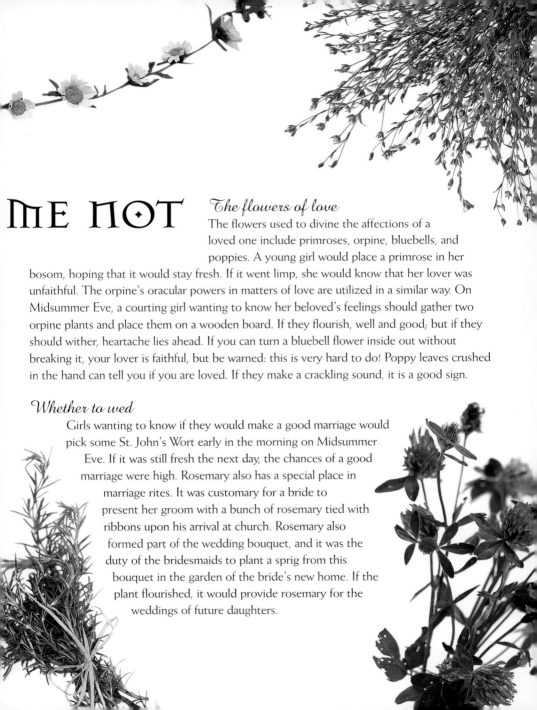

# ME NOT

## The flowers of love

The flowers used to divine the affections of a loved one include primroses, orpine, bluebells, and poppies. A young girl would place a primrose in her bosom, hoping that it would stay fresh. If it went limp, she would know that her lover was unfaithful. The orpine's oracular powers in matters of love are utilized in a similar way. On Midsummer Eve, a courting girl wanting to know her beloved's feelings should gather two orpine plants and place them on a wooden board. If they flourish, well and good; but if they should wither, heartache lies ahead. If you can turn a bluebell flower inside out without breaking it, your lover is faithful, but be warned: this is very hard to do! Poppy leaves crushed in the hand can tell you if you are loved. If they make a crackling sound, it is a good sign.

## Whether to wed

Girls wanting to know if they would make a good marriage would pick some St. John's Wort early in the morning on Midsummer Eve. If it was still fresh the next day, the chances of a good marriage were high. Rosemary also has a special place in marriage rites. It was customary for a bride to present her groom with a bunch of rosemary tied with ribbons upon his arrival at church. Rosemary also formed part of the wedding bouquet, and it was the duty of the bridesmaids to plant a sprig from this bouquet in the garden of the bride's new home. If the plant flourished, it would provide rosemary for the weddings of future daughters.

# chapter two
# APHRODITE'S SECRETS

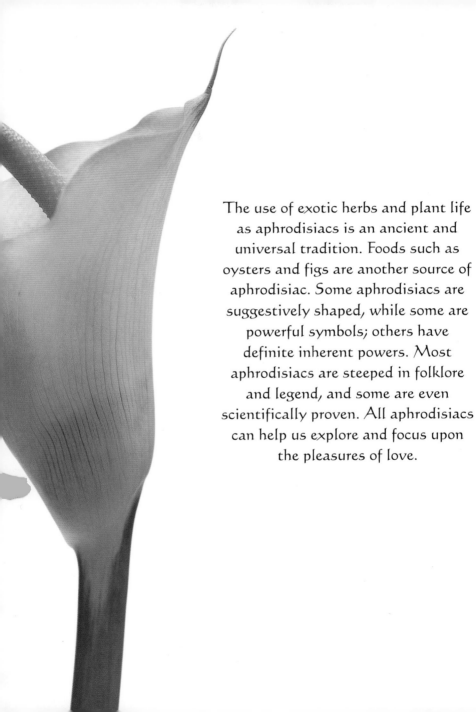

The use of exotic herbs and plant life as aphrodisiacs is an ancient and universal tradition. Foods such as oysters and figs are another source of aphrodisiac. Some aphrodisiacs are suggestively shaped, while some are powerful symbols; others have definite inherent powers. Most aphrodisiacs are steeped in folklore and legend, and some are even scientifically proven. All aphrodisiacs can help us explore and focus upon the pleasures of love.

# FRUITY SALAD

*A luscious salad full of
delicious, sensuous fruits*

## YOU WILL NEED

## YOU WILL NEED

*selection of your
favorite fruits*

*half of a lime*

*dextrose (fruit sugar)*

*goat's (or sheep's)
yogurt*

*thick, clear honey*

*pine nuts*

Ripe, juicy fruits have had a sexual connotation ever since Eve tempted Adam with an apple. Many other fruits have traditionally had a reputation as aphrodisiacs, or have been used as erotic symbols, including peaches, fresh figs, bananas, cherries, and mangoes. Many of these fruits contain significant amounts of phenylethylamine, the pleasure-inducing hormone released during sex. Apart from their wonderful taste and texture, mangoes are attributed with aphrodisiac properties. Bananas are obviously phallic, and figs have their own sexual connotations. Peaches, too, are highly suggestive. Watching the object of your desire eat a luscious fruit, passing cherries from mouth to mouth, or exchanging peach or mango kisses are the pastimes of Eros and Venus. One of the best ways to combine all the pleasures of fruit is to make a salad of your favorites. Here is an outstanding recipe which includes honey, pine nuts, and yogurt, all of which are celebrated in the classic Arabian love manual *The Perfumed Garden*.

## METHOD

Cut a selection of freshly washed fruit into chunks or slices. Add the juice of half of a lime and mix in a bowl. Sprinkle lightly with dextrose (fruit sugar) and refrigerate for at least an hour, preferably two. The dextrose will draw some of the juice out of the fruit. Stir in as much yogurt as you wish, dribble on some thick, clear honey, and top with a handful of pine nuts. Indulge.

# DAMIANA

*A powerful potion to cure frigidity
and melt the heart of your beloved*

## YOU WILL NEED

1 tbsp (15ml)
damiana leaves

1 tbsp (15ml) saw
palmetto berries,
powdered

1 tbsp (15ml) wild
oats

1 tbsp (15ml) honey

1 pint (½L) water

Damiana is a pretty flowering plant native to Mexico. It is named after St. Damian, the patron saint of pharmacists. It was used by the pre-Columbian peoples of Mexico, including the Maya and Aztecs, as both an aphrodisiac and a remedy for asthma. It is as an aphrodisiac, however, that damiana's fame has spread around the world. Traditionally, it was used to remedy frigidity in women and impotence in men, working as a stimulant tonic on the reproductive system of both sexes. It was also used in the tantric sex magic practices of certain occult groups that flourished from the late 19th century onward. For best results, damiana should be taken in moderation over a reasonable period of time: at least two months. Thereafter, take it only during the waxing moon. Do not be tempted to take more than the dosage suggested below, as excessive doses can be harmful to the liver. Damiana can be taken in many ways: smoked, macerated in alcohol, or in capsules, where it is mixed with wild oats or saw palmetto berries. It can also be imbibed as a tea. The following formula is suited to both men and women.

## METHOD

Place the damiana leaves, saw palmetto berries, and wild oats in a pan. Add the water and honey and bring to the boil. Cover and simmer gently for five minutes. Divide into three doses and take morning, noon, and night.

# CHASTE TREE

*To excite your passion
and stimulate your love*

## YOU WILL NEED

*1 tsp (5ml) ripe
chaste tree berries*

*honey (optional)*

Chaste tree, or *Agnus castus,* is an aromatic shrub with
pretty palmate leaves and spikes of scented lilac flowers.
The small, peppercorn-like berries have a reputation for both
stimulating and reducing sexual desire. The great Roman
doctor Dioscorides relates that during the Greek festival
known as the Thesmophoria, during which the women would
rebel against the men, married women would strew the bed
with chaste tree berries, to discourage their husbands. As
well, legend has it that temple priestesses in ancient Greece
and Rome would take the berries to lessen desire. Recent
evidence suggests, however, that the berries actually have
the opposite effect on women. Indeed, in the tree's native
southern Europe, they have a long-established reputation as
a female aphrodisiac. It seems that the plant corrects
hormonal imbalances, keeping the libido at optimum levels.
Chaste tree can be safely used over a long period, but
excessive quantities can cause nervous disorders.

## METHOD

Pour boiling water over one teaspoon of chaste tree berries.
Allow to steep for ten to fifteen minutes. Drink with honey, if
desired, first thing in the morning and twice more during the
day. The tea is pleasantly pungent with a bittersweet taste.

# Sarsaparilla

*A delicious and refreshing love tonic to help you capture the heart of the partner you covet*

## You will need

*1 oz (30g) sarsaparilla*

*1 oz (30g) sassafras*

*1 oz (30g) ginseng*

*5 pints (3L) water*

*8 oz (225g) honey or sugar*

*1–2 tsp (5–10ml) brewer's or baker's yeast*

*bottles*

*bottle caps or corks*

The indigenous peoples of the New World have been using the roots of sarsaparilla for centuries as a tonic for general weakness, as well as to improve sexual performance. Sarsaparilla contains some important sex hormones, including testosterone and progesterone, as well as other chemicals that assist the activity of such hormones. There are many varieties of sarsaparilla; those with the deeper reddish-orange roots are considered the best. A great way to ingest sarsaparilla is as a root beer made with sassafras and ginseng. Sassafras is considered a sacred medicine tree by the natives of North America, and is particularly venerated as a tree of love. Here it assists the alterative effects of sarsaparilla and has a great taste, while the ginseng boosts the tonic effect.

## Method

Boil the sarsaparilla, sassafras, and ginseng together in water for twenty minutes. Strain, add the honey or sugar, and allow to cool. Add the brewer's or baker's yeast, cover, and leave in a warm room. After a couple of hours, small bubbles should have started to appear, indicating that fermentation has begun. Decant into bottles and cap or cork tightly. Store in a cool place or refrigerate. Wait a day before drinking.

# LOVE SALAD

*A salacious selection of
vegetables with erotic potency*

## You will need

*selection of salad
vegetables*

*vinaigrette dressing*

*fresh basil*

*garlic bread*

*goat's cheese*

*roasted pine nuts*

*whole celery stalks*

Many lovers find eating together an erotic experience: no wonder a romantic date usually involves a good meal as a prelude to further pleasure! All vegetables are, of course, full of vitamins and minerals. They are regular powerhouses of natural energy, rapidly boosting our resources. In addition, many vegetables also have reputations as libido enhancers, owing either to their suggestive shape or their chemistry. Fennel, in particular, has been enjoyed as an erotic stimulant since ancient times, and not just due to its bulbous shape. Avocados, artichokes, lettuce, endive, leeks, tomatoes, onions, and garlic all have long-standing reputations as love foods, and it has recently been established that celery may encourage the release of sex hormones. All beans have libidinous reputations, as do mushrooms—especially truffles. The best way to eat most of these love foods is when they are raw, and the best way to eat vegetables raw is in a salad.

## METHOD

Prepare a selection of your favorite vegetables and toss them in a salad bowl with a vinaigrette dressing. Add any or all of the following love foods: fresh basil; goat's cheese, cubed or crumbled; and roasted pine nuts. Serve with garlic bread and whole celery stalks. Be sure to discuss the attributes of the ingredients with those who are sharing the meal.

# HORNY GOAT WEED

*An ancient Chinese herb with
extraordinary aphrodisiacal powers*

## YOU WILL NEED

2 oz (60g) horny
goat weed

white tequila

mortar and pestle

glass jar

dark glass bottle

Traditional Chinese medicine represents the oldest unbroken medical tradition in the world. The *Huang Ti Nei Qing Su Wen* (Yellow Emperor's Classic of Internal Medicine) dates back, at least in part, to the Shang dynasty (c. 1523–1028 BC), making it the oldest medical textbook in existence. This and other ancient Chinese medical texts list thousands of different plants and recipes. One plant that was kept secret for many centuries was the splendidly named horny goat weed (*epimedium* species, particularly *epimedium sagittatum*). This mountain herb is considered one of the most powerful plant aphrodisiacs, and is currently undergoing scientific tests in the West for its powers to cure impotence, frigidity, frequent urination, forgetfulness, and menstrual irregularity associated with hypertension. The dried herb (also called *yin yang huo*) can be obtained from Chinese herbalists or by mail order. The best day to use the weed is a Tuesday, preferably during the waxing moon. Here is a recipe for a tincture made from this herb.

## METHOD

Grind some dried horny goat weed to a powder, place in a glass jar, and cover with white tequila. Place somewhere warm and dark for two weeks. Strain into a dark glass bottle. Place seven drops of the mixture in warm water and drink three times a day before meals as a tonic. As with all herbs, it is best to take a break of a week or so after an intial two month period.

# CHOCOLATE LOVE BALLS

*A delectable dessert
with an amorous twist*

## You will need

*3 oz (90g) chocolate*

*1 oz (30g) brown
sugar*

*3 oz (90g) raw honey*

*8 oz (225g) flour*

*pinch of nutmeg*

*pinch of cinnamon*

*1 tsp (5ml) ground
ginger*

*1 tsp (5ml)
bicarbonate of soda*

*1 tbsp (15ml) warm
water*

*½ oz (15g) stem or
crystallized ginger,
chopped*

*½ oz (15g) pine nuts,
chopped*

Chocolate has been one of the world's favorite love foods ever since it was brought back from Mexico by the conquistadors. The Aztecs had been steeped in the culture of chocolate for longer than anyone knows. The emperor Montezuma was said to have drunk as many as fifty cups of chocolate a day, to help him service his demanding harem. Modern science refuted chocolate's reputation as an aphrodisiac until recently, when studies conducted at the New York State Psychiatric Institute showed that chocolate releases phenylethylamine, the same pleasure hormone that is released during sex. It is true that you would have to eat a lot of chocolate in order to consume what might be considered an aphrodisiacal dose, but every little bit helps. Here is a recipe for romantic success which combines chocolate with other notorious libido boosters.

## Method

Place the chocolate, brown sugar, and honey in a pan and stand it over a low heat until the contents have melted. Sift the flour, the nutmeg and cinnamon, and the ground ginger into a bowl. Add bicarbonate of soda combined with warm water, the melted chocolate mixture, the ginger, and the pine nuts. Mix well, then shape into about twenty-four small balls. Place on a buttered baking tray, allowing room for spreading. Bake at 350°F (180°C) for fifteen minutes. When cooled, store the balls in an airtight container—if you can keep your hands off of them.

# Yohimbe

*One of the most potent aphrodisiacs in the world, yohimbe is the ultimate sensual journey*

## You will need

½ tsp (2g) of
yohimbe bark

1½ tsp (2g) of
ginseng

1 cup (250ml)
spring water

4 limes

1 tbsp (15ml) honey

Yohimbe is a tall evergreen tree native to West Africa. For centuries, the Bantu-speaking tribes of that region have used the bark as an aphrodisiac, to sustain them through orgiastic marriage rituals. Yohimbe is the only plant considered by the orthodox medical establishment to be a true aphrodisiac. It increases the flow of blood to the erogenous zones and, by constricting the veins, helps to keep it there. Effective for both men and women, it can also increase desire and sensitivity. Yohimbe should be used with caution. Its effects can be long-lasting—two to four hours usually, but sometimes longer, during which time sleep can be impossible. It can produce such side effects as nausea and, in large doses, high blood pressure and hallucinations. It should thus be avoided by people with circulation or blood pressure problems, diabetes, ulcers, or kidney disorders. It should not be taken with prescription drugs, nor in conjunction with cheese, liver, or alcohol. For a healthy person, however, the occasional moderate use of yohimbe should present no problem. The following is a safe, effective love potion.

## Method

Place the yohimbe bark and ginseng in a pan. Boil the spring water and add it to the pan, along with honey and the juice of four limes. Boil until the liquid is reduced to half. Allow to cool, then add more honey to taste.

# LOVE BUNS

*An offering of tantalizing buns
to entice and arouse your beloved*

## YOU WILL NEED

*2 lb (925g) plain flour*

*3 oz (90g) caster sugar*

*1 oz (30g) yeast*

*4 oz (125g) lukewarm
goat's milk*

*4 tbsp (60ml) water*

*1 tsp (5ml) salt*

*1 tsp (5ml) mixed
spices (ginger,
nutmeg, coriander)*

*½ tsp (2.5ml)
cinnamon*

*8 oz (225g) currants*

*2 oz (60g) pine nuts*

*2 oz (60g) butter*

*1 egg, beaten*

*2 oz (60g) sugar*

*3 tbsp (45ml) milk*

This recipe utilizes various spices famed for their libidinous qualities. Use your hands when mixing the ingredients, and try to focus on the object of your desire. If you like, say a little spell or make a wish as you prepare the food.

## METHOD

Sift 4 oz (125g) of flour into a bowl and add 1 tsp (5ml) of caster sugar. Blend the yeast with the goat's milk and water and add to the flour and sugar. Mix well and leave for twenty to thirty minutes, or until frothy. Meanwhile, sift 1¾ lb (800g) of flour with the salt, mixed spice, and cinnamon into another bowl. Add 2 oz (60g) of caster sugar and the currants and pine nuts. Toss lightly together. Add to the yeast mixture with the butter and egg. Mix to a soft dough that leaves the side of the bowl clean. Turn out onto a floured board and knead for five minutes (or until the dough is smooth and not sticky). While kneading, be sure to transfer your wishes to the food through your fingers. Cover the dough and leave to rise until it doubles in size. Imagine that the dough is swelling with your desires. Turn out onto a freshly floured board. Knead lightly and divide into twelve round shapes. Place well apart on a lightly buttered and floured baking tray. Cover and leave to rise for thirty minutes. Bake at 425°F (220°C) for twenty to twenty-five minutes. Transfer the buns to a wire rack. Brush twice with glaze made by dissolving sugar in milk and boiling for two minutes. Offer a bun to the lover you covet.

# Muira Puama

*A powerful tonic to prepare
you for love*

## You will need

2 oz (60g) muira
puama

1 pint (½L) white
rum or vodka

8 oz (225g) honey

glass bottle

Muira puama is a small tree that grows mainly in the Brazilian Amazon. Indigenous tribes in Brazil use the roots and bark to make a tea for treating sexual debility and impotency, neuromuscular problems, rheumatism, and to prevent baldness. Early European explorers noted its aphrodisiac qualities and brought it back to Europe. It is now used throughout the world, and has been gaining popularity in the United States, where herbalists and health care practitioners are using it for impotency, menstrual cramps and pre-menstrual syndrome, neurasthenia, and central nervous system disorders. Two recent case studies showed that muira puama is effective in improving libido. In order to benefit from its full effects, the herb must be prepared correctly, as the oils and resins found in the root and bark are not easily digested. Here is the best way to use the herb.

## Method

Put the muira puama in a pan with a close-fitting lid. Pour the white rum or vodka and the honey over it. Cover, and slowly bring to just below boiling point. Allow to infuse for twenty minutes without boiling. Let cool. Strain into a glass bottle. To avoid having to drink the alcohol, you can make the brew with-out fitting the lid, in which case most of the alcohol will evaporate, but you will also lose some of the volatile oils. Take 3 tsp (15ml) in water three times a day, or a good shot an hour or two before amorous encounters.

# PAELLA PUELLA

*From Spain, a libidinous savory
dish featuring the fruits of the sea*

## You will need

3 tbsp (45ml) olive oil

chopped garlic clove

pinch of saffron

1 onion, chopped

4 oz (125g) squid

2 small tomatoes,
peeled and quartered

8 oz (225g) long-
grain rice

15 tbsp (225ml) fish
stock

8 asparagus spears

lobster tail, white
fish cut into pieces

handful of prawns

3 de-shelled oysters

handful of mussels

parsley or cilantro

Paella is a Spanish rice dish that has become famous throughout the world. It is delicious in all its different guises, but one reason for its popularity may be the fact that it contains so many ingredients which have a reputation for supporting and enhancing the libido. This recipe is a variation of a "Paella Valenciana," and contains seafood—creatures "from the foam," like Aphrodite herself. The name of this dish, Paella, comes from the iron frying pan with two handles in which the rice is cooked and served. *Puella* is Latin for girl.

## METHOD

Heat the olive oil in a deep iron frying pan or a paella pan and add the garlic. Add the onion and the squid. When the onion is transparent, add the tomatoes. Stir in the rice and cook gently for five minutes. Cover with well-seasoned fish stock, to which a pinch of saffron has been added. Add the asparagus spears. Cook for five minutes more, then add the white fish, lobster tail, prawns, oysters, and mussels. Boil hard for five minutes, then simmer until the rice is moist but not soupy, adding more stock as necessary. Place the paella in the oven for a few minutes at 400°F (200°C). Sprinkle with fresh chopped parsley or cilantro.

# SAW PALMETTO

*A multi-purpose herb for enhancing the
libido and maintaining a healthy sex life*

## YOU WILL NEED

*1 oz (30g) saw
palmetto berries,
ground*

*1 oz (30g) ginseng*

*1 pint (½L) brandy*

*dark glass bottle*

The saw palmetto is a small palm tree that grows on the Atlantic and Gulf coasts of the United States. In traditional Chinese medicine, the berries are considered a powerful tonic for both yang and yin (male and female energies), helping to balance the hormones in both men and women. Saw palmetto has recently gained popularity as a remedy for prostate problems in men. In the opinion of many medical herbalists, all men over the age of forty would do well to take saw palmetto regularly to protect and support the functioning of the prostate. Saw palmetto is also one of the most useful, safe, and adaptable of all the herbs that have a direct action on the reproductive system. The berries can boost the libido, and help overcome impotence and frigidity. It mixes well with other herbs—horsetail and echinacea for prostate problems, damiana as an aphrodisiac, and muira puama as a long-term libido tonic. Here is a recipe for keeping yourself and the man or woman in your life in peak condition.

## METHOD

Cover the saw palmetto berries and ginseng with the brandy, preferably during a new moon. Cover and keep in a warm, dark place for two weeks. Filter into a dark glass bottle. Take 2tsp (10ml) in water once a day. Take a break of about fourteen days every few months.

# Wild Oats

*Drink this arousing tonic,
then go sow your wild oats*

## You will need

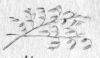

*wild green oats*

*juicer*

*high-proof alcohol*

We are all familiar with the terms "sowing wild oats" and "getting your oats". Not surprising, then, to discover that wild green oats really are an important love tonic. They help release testosterone, the primary sex hormone in both males and females, allowing it to boost the libido. Desire, sensation, and performance can be enhanced in both men and women. Wild green oats are known to work well in support of other sexual tonics, such as saw palmetto, damiana, and muira puama. They are widely available in extract form from nutritionists as *avena sativa* (the Latin for oat), which can be taken as a daily health supplement. The best way to get your wild oats, however, is in their fresh, natural state.

## Method

Pick wild oats anywhere you find them, so long as they are not too near a source of pollution. They are best picked from spring until early summer, while they are green and flowing with milky sap. Put them through a juicer and drink 6 tbsp (90ml) once or twice a day. The juice will keep for three to four days, as long as it is refrigerated. Each time you juice the oats, collect the residue from the juicer and cover it in high-proof alcohol for a few days. Strain and keep the green tincture. After three extractions, it will be quite potent, and can be taken in place of the juice. Take 1 tsp (5ml) in warm water two or three times a day. If you wish to avoid the alcohol, take it in hot water—most of the alcohol will evaporate.

The ultimate secret

# ○CEAΠS
## ○F

According to legend, Venus (or, in
Greek mythology, Aphrodite), the
guide and inspiration of all lovers,
emerged naked and glorious from the
sea. Because of this legend, the
ocean has always been viewed as a
powerful symbol and source of love
and desire.

# L⊙VE

## Oysters and shellfish

Of all the creatures in the sea, oysters have the greatest reputation as an aphrodisiac—after all, it was an oyster shell that brought forth Venus. The sensual appearance of raw oysters on the half-shell combined with their fresh, tangy taste make them highly suggestive, while their rich proteins and minerals provide a quick boost of energy, satisfying one appetite and restoring another. Casanova, the archetypal lover, was a great believer in the amatory powers of oysters—he is reputed to have breakfasted on as many as fifty at a time while bathing with his lovers. Other shellfish, including cockles, clams, scallops, and the wickedly-shaped mussel, also have reputations as foods of love.

## Of fish and fugu

The roe (eggs) of all fish are considered particularly efficacious aphrodisiacs. Fresh sea urchin roe is delicious and highly prized, as, of course, is caviar. Legend has it that in order to provide the heir that her husband could not, Catherine the Great (a woman of legendary libido) summoned a strong, handsome officer of the Royal Guard to dinner and plied him with caviar. Russia's heir was assured that night. Even sturgeon, from which caviar is taken, has an aphrodisiac reputation.

Generally speaking, all fish are considered libido enhancers. Anchovies, eels, halibut, mackerel, plaice, salmon, and skate are particularly noted for their potency.

Possibly the most infamous ocean aphrodisiac is the fugu, a type of puffer fish highly prized by the Japanese. The skin and various organs of this fish contain a lethal poison, and only after several years' training can a chef receive a license to serve this deadly delicacy.

To eschew the fruits of the sea is to eschew some of the most deliciously visceral pleasures of love. Sample the effects for yourself and you can be sure of the approval of foam-flecked Venus.

*chapter three*

# THE
# PERFUMED

The sense of smell and the exuding of special scents are crucial to the mating game of all plants and animals, and we humans are no exception. Flowers attract us with their scent and beauty, and are used by poets and artists as the principle metaphor for love. Spices, too, are exotic and erotic, intriguing and delighting us with their smell and taste. Here we learn how deeply the treasures of nature's garden can affect us.

# GARDEN

# Frankincense and Myrhh

*A luxurious lotion to
rejuvenate body and soul*

## You will need

*2 tsp (10ml) evening
primrose oil*

*4 tsp (20ml)
grapeseed oil*

*essential oils of
frankincense, myrrh,
and rose absolute*

*dark glass bottle*

Frankincense and myrhh are both aromatic resins produced by tough little trees growing in the deserts of Arabia. Along with gold, they have always been considered gifts fit for gods and monarchs. The three wise men bore these gifts to the infant Jesus, while the Queen of England is presented with them every year on the Feast of Epiphany. Ancient Egyptian, Greek, and Biblical texts as much as 6,000 years old mention their use as medicines and in religious and magical rites. Indeed, myrrh was the primary ingredient of a holy anointing oil that the Lord bade Moses rub on his body before approaching the Tabernacle. To this day, frankincense and myrrh are used all over the world to cleanse, purify, and protect. They are also used as ingredients in love potions, and the smell of frankincense has been shown to have an aphrodisiac effect on men. It is in cosmetics, though, that these precious resins are finding a new and special place: they seem to have the ability to rejuvenate the skin, improving tone and removing fine lines. Here is an exquisite elixir of youth that Cleopatra would have envied.

## Method

Blend the evening primrose oil and grapeseed oil with five drops each of frankincense and myrrh essential oils and rose absolute. Apply nightly for a luxurious and rejuvenating facial massage. The potion is also wonderful for the body when applied to damp skin. If stored in a dark glass bottle, it will last six months.

# PERENNIAL LOVE

*Plant these flowers and the seeds
of your love will never die*

## You will need

*periwinkle plants or
seeds*

The pretty periwinkle holds a special place in the lexicon of love. It was considered to have aphrodisiac qualities in ancient times. The medieval alchemist Albertus Magnus prescribed a strange recipe in his *Boke of Secretes* involving periwinkles and earthworms, insisting that "it induce the love between man and wyfe if it bee used in their meales." Nicholas Culpepper echoed this 400 years later, writing that the leaves eaten "by a man and wife cause love between them." Happily, he dispenses with the earthworms. Today, the periwinkle has a distinctive place in herbal medicine: it is considered a great binder and an excellent astringent. It is also considered useful in treating diabetes. The Madagascar periwinkle has achieved fame as a cancer cure, an indication of how powerful this species can be. The periwinkle gets its name from the Latin *vincio*—to bind—and *perennis*—ever. Thus, the "everbind" (its main magical indication) can help bind couples forever. Here is a way to stay happily coupled always.

## METHOD

Periwinkle is a beautiful plant with pretty violet flowers. It is perennial, meaning that its glossy green leaves survive the winter. It was once called "joy of the ground," which shows how much it was appreciated as a ground cover. A couple can help to ensure a long and happy partnership by planting periwinkle in the garden of their home.

# PERSIAN ENCHANTMENT

*A ritual from the harem to capture your
lover's heart, body, and soul*

## You will need

*These essential oils
should always be
used diluted 1:5 or
1:10 in a base oil
such as grapeseed*

essential oils of
gardenia, rose,
peppermint,
patchouli, and lilac

honey

ambergris

almond milk

vetiver or musk
(synthetic)

Passed down by princesses from generation to generation,
this sophisticated ritual uses some of the world's most
precious and alluring scents. Do not undertake such a potent
charm lightly—its results are usually irreversible.

## METHOD

On the head of she who will choose, a drop of gardenia to catch the
zephyr and float to him whom she would choose.

On the eyelids of she who will choose, a drop of rose oil to entice him
whom she would choose.

On her mouth, a drop of honey, to soften the mouth of him whom she
would choose.

On her tongue, a drop of peppermint, to spark the flame in the loins
of him whom she would choose.

On her neck, a drop of ambergris, to give the flush of heat to him
whom she would choose.

On each breast, a drop of almond milk, to nourish him whom she
would choose.

On her stomach, a drop of vetiver to awaken lust in him whom she
would choose.

On her mound of mirth, a drop of patchouli to unleash the throbbing
serpent in him whom she would choose.

On the lips of her maiden flower, a drop of lilac to lick for him
whom she would choose.

For when these drops are combined with her lover's milk of passion,
their union inside her will bring the fruit of happiness and long life.

74

# FLOWER CHARM

*A floral bouquet to beckon
the lover of your dreams*

## You will need

*six red roses*

*five white roses*

*two white lilies*

*one tiger lily*

*large vase*

With their delicate grace and beauty and lovely scents, flowers have long been symbols of the feminine principle. They use their charms to attract the bees to pollinate them and ensure that they will bear seed. In this respect, they symbolize seduction and fertility. Certain flowers are associated with love and romance, including roses, lilies, and orchids, all of which are ruled by Venus. Roses are probably the most widely recognized symbol of love. Red roses suggest passionate, romantic love; pink roses suggest affection; while white roses are emblems of pure, idealized love. The lily is generally a symbol of purity and virginity, and is sacred to all virgin goddesses, but the Madonna lily, with its phallic stigma, symbolizes sex and fecundity, and the tiger lily says "I dare you to love me." Orchids symbolize love, harmony, refinement, beauty, and femininity. Here is a flower charm that expresses potential availability, dependent upon true love and respect.

## METHOD

In a large vase mingle six red roses, signifying man and passion, with five white roses, symbolizing woman and pure love. On either side place a single white lily as protection from the virgin goddesses. At the back of the bunch place a glamorous tiger lily, to challenge a man or woman to love you as you deserve.

# Spice it up

*Add zest to your sex life with these two
delicious concoctions of amorous ingredients*

## You will need

chocolate ice cream

milk

chocolate sauce

cinnamon essence

1 tsp (5ml) ground
coriander

1 tsp (5ml) ground
ginger

fresh black pepper

a handful of
strawberries,
preferably wild

strawberry ice cream

blender

We are most familiar with spices for their culinary virtues, but for thousands of years they have been valued just as highly for their medicinal properties. Ginger, for example, stimulates the circulation, and is a reputed aphrodisiac. Cinnamon excites sexual response in women. Other libido enhancers include aniseed, cloves, cardamom, cumin, coriander, fennel seeds, nutmeg, pepper, and vanilla. Some spices combine superbly with milk and ice cream—these are ideal in summertime for cooling the body and inflaming the passions. Use spice essences, as they mix better with cold milk; otherwise, grind the spices and let them stand in warm milk for a few minutes before refrigerating. Here are two refreshing and stimulating shakes.

## Method

### Cinnamon Girl

Blend chocolate ice cream with milk, real chocolate sauce, and cinnamon essence for a sensational milkshake.

### Venus and Mars

This delicious potion combines coriander and strawberries (representing Venus) with ginger and black pepper (representing Mars) to forge the union of heaven's most passionate couple. Stand the ground coriander and ginger in a cup of warm milk for five minutes. Refrigerate for an hour. Blend the strawberries with the spicy milk, strawberry ice cream, and black pepper.

# FLOWER GARLAND

*A simple celebration of
the stirrings of the heart*

## YOU WILL NEED

*18 in (45cm) length
of ivy*

*selection of flowers*

*slender ribbons or
thin wire*

*sharp knife*

*tweezers*

In the past, young girls would wear garlands of flowers as an expression of their readiness for love, and various flowers came to represent different nuances of love. An awareness of these qualities can help us focus on the nature of our intent.

### FLOWERS AND THEIR MEANINGS

*Blue sage says "I think of you."*
*Daisies are ruled by Venus and express the hope for true love.*
*Heartsease or wild pansies symbolize a heart touched by love.*
*Periwinkles are sacred to Venus and symbolize early friendship.*
*Primroses are ruled by Venus and represent young love.*
*Roses mean love in any language. Red roses suggest passionate love, white roses platonic love, and rosebuds suggest innocence.*
*Summer savory is suggestive of desire.*
*Violets are sacred to Venus and represent affection and faithfulness.*

## METHOD

To weave a garland, cut a length of young ivy with small leaves. Using a sharp knife, cut little slits in the stalk, just large enough to pass a flower stem through. Use tweezers to hold the slit open, and insert the flower of your choice. While weaving the garland, incant a wish. Secure with a slender ribbon or thin wire if necessary. Continue thus until the ivy is threaded with as many flowers as you wish, then bind the ends together with wire or ribbon and place carefully upon your head. Repeat your incantation three times to confirm your wish.

# Sweet Soul Oils

*An arousing
blend of sweet oils*

## You will need

*essential oils of
ginger, cinnamon,
clove, and lavender*

*incense burner*

The alchemists believe that everything manifest in the universe consists of three principles: soul, spirit, and body. The spirit is life force, the body is material form, and the soul is the individuality or essence of a thing. In the plant world, the soul principle of a plant resides in its essential oil. This is what most clearly differentiates it from other plants. The unmistakable aromas of cinnamon, jasmine, or lavender come from their essential oils. These smells all trigger different effects within us: some are calming, some are energizing, and some are arousing. This is the basis of aromatherapy, an ancient art which has achieved enormous popularity in recent years. The mechanisms that cause the effects of essential oils are subtle, yet penetrating. They can transform our mood, and with regular use, can effect gradual transformations within us. The best ways to use them are in the bath, in incense burners, and in massage oils. Essential oils are extremely concentrated, and thus should never be applied directly to the skin; they should be mixed with a mild base oil like almond, grapeseed, or avocado oil. Here is one blend of oils which has proven exceptionally arousing.

## Method

Fill the evaporating dish of an incense burner half full with water and add three drops each of ginger and cinnamon oils, one of clove oil, and two of lavender oil. Set to burn in the bedroom half an hour before going to bed.

# Wildflower Passion Posy

*A ritual summoning the amatory powers of Venus and Mars*

## You will need

selection of
Venusian and
Martial flowers

small vases or posy
pots

ribbon, string, or
rubber bands

Venus and Mars are the divine celestial lovers. Voluptuous Venus represents the more feminine aspects of love—affection, comfort, and pleasure. Fiery Mars is her masculine counterpart, the passionate, highly sexual warrior. Together, they epitomize the principle that opposites attract. In alchemy, these divine planetary bodies rule the plants of love. Many of these plants produce lovely flowers.

The following flowers are ruled by Venus: *columbine (aquilegia vulgaris), primula species (including cowslips and primroses), mallows (malva and althaea species), lilies, roses, orchids, periwinkles, self-heal (prunella vulgaris), yarrow (achillea), violets, and cherry blossom.*
The following flowers are ruled by Mars: *Hedge hyssop (gratiola), pasque flower (pulsatilla), anemones, buttercups, sweet basil, thistles, tobacco (nicotiana tabacum), toadflax (linaria vulgaris), and broom (cytisus scoparius).*

## Method

Combine a mixture of Venusian and Martial flowers of similar size. Trim the stems and leaves, then arrange a series of bunches in small vases or posy pots. Place in all of the rooms where you and your lover meet, particularly the bedroom. Posies can also be tied with ribbon, string, or rubber bands and given to your lover. You can use ornamental varieties of any of the species mentioned, but the wild varieties tend to have stronger spirits.

Sealed potion ☞

# Mandrake Love Charm

*Plant these seeds and
watch love bloom*

*mandrake seed*

One fascinating aspect of mandrake is that its root is considered to resemble the shape of a man or woman. In some parts of the world, the most suggestively shaped roots are kept or sold as magical dolls or love charms. The plant in question is the Old World species (*mandragora officinarum*), not to be confused with American mandrake (*podophyllum peltatum*). Mandrake is too rare a plant to pick, but its seeds are available. With care and patience, you can grow your own and use it as a love charm.

## Method

Prepare a plot at least 2 ft 6 in (85cm) square. On the first Wednesday of the new moon in Aries, plant a single seed 1 in (25mm) deep. Make sure the soil remains moist until germination occurs. Establish a relationship with the plant as it grows. Honor and respect it. Tell it that when it is ready, you will deliver it into a new existence. Shortly before sunset on the Wednesday closest to the ninth full moon following, excavate the root very carefully, facing westward as you work. Do not remove the root before sunset. Bring it into the house and place it in a lukewarm bath. Wash it very carefully and tenderly, rinse it with cold water, and pat it dry with a towel. Hang it root downward in a warm, dry place, out of direct sunlight. Allow it to dry out. Keep it in a cupboard or on a mantelpiece. Treated as a conscious being, it can help mediate your wishes, particularly in matters of love and fertility.

# LOVE-IN-A-MIST

*Plant this flower in your garden
and your beloved will be faithful*

## YOU WILL NEED

*love-in-a-mist seeds
or plants*

This charming folk name is applied to two different plants that are closely related. The first, *Nigella damascena*, is a delicate, fairy-like flower, most commonly grown as an ornamental. It is an annual, growing anew from seed each year. It has a lovely cobalt blue flower surrounded by sprays of deeply cut, fine lacy leaves. The leaves create a wonderful, hazy effect—hence the name. The crowned seedpod, an attractive feature of the plant, is used in dried flower arrangements, and the seed may be sprinkled on bread or cookies. Its sister, with which it shares its name, is *Nigella sativa*. This plant also has very pretty flowers, usually purple, but with less delicate foliage. Both types of love-in-a-mist are self-seeding, and are hardy enough to grow in northern latitudes. In parts of Europe, *Nigella damascena* was planted in the garden to ensure fidelity in a relationship.

## METHOD

If you wish for your lover to remain faithful, plant love-in-a-mist in your garden. Tend to it well, for if it thrives, your sweetheart will be true. Be sure to sprinkle some of the seeds from the seedpods onto the earth; if it comes up again in the spring, you can take this as a sign that your relationship will last.

# Animal Magnet

*Wear the scent of love to
attract the object of your desire*

## You will need

*essential oils of
bergamot, orange,
rose absolute,
jasmine absolute,
patchouli, vanilla,
myrrh, galbanum,
sandalwood, and
clary sage*

*2 tbsp (30ml)
grapeseed oil*

*dark glass bottle*

Many animals produce distinctive scents to mark their
territory and attract mates. Some have been greatly sought
after as ingredients in perfume and as aphrodisiacs. Extracts
from the pungent scent glands of the musk, a small deer
found in Tibet and China, the civet cat from Africa, and the
beaver from Canada and Siberia, were used for centuries for
these purposes. In some places, the deeply arousing scent of
musk was considered morally corrupting; Pope Pius the
Faithful threatened merchants with excommunication for
handling it, while in England, a bill was laid before
Parliament ruling that "any woman who used musk to gain a
proposal should have her marriage annulled." In recent
decades, bowing to pressure from animal rights groups, the
perfume industry has gone to great lengths to derive these
animal scents from plant sources such as clary sage and
tobacco. Today, natural non-animal scents can be used to
make "chypre," an exotic perfume blend of legendary powers.
Here is a chypre blend that you can make yourself.

## Method

In a dark glass bottle mix two drops each of bergamot, orange,
rose absolute, jasmine absolute, patchouli, vanilla, myrrh, and
galbanum essential oils with five drops each of sandalwood and
clary sage. Add the grapeseed oil, then blend well for a
perfumed oil of rare delight.

The most intoxicating perfume

# BODILY LOVE

Everybody appreciates a sensual, soothing body massage, and there are few things more pleasurable than a lover's sure and gentle touch. Massage is a wonderful way to show your love, and to bring healing and pleasure at the same time. It is also a superb way to arouse and seduce.

## Fragrant oils

The tactile pleasure of loving hands on skin is greatly enhanced by the use of oils, especially when mixed with exotic essential oils. The best massage oils are pure vegetable oils, the lightest of which are grapeseed and coconut. Sweet almond oil is the favorite medium oil; avocado and olive oil are are a bit heavier, but work just as well. Vegetable oils have one potential drawback, however; they are not latex-friendly. A wonderful alternative is ghee—clarified butter—which the skin adores. Jojoba and cocoa butter are also rich and penetrating.

When added to a base oil and massaged into the skin, essential oils will be absorbed by the body, and can have a profoundly relaxing and sensual effect. The essences most noted for their libido-enhancing qualities include ylang ylang, sandalwood, jasmine, clary sage, rose, bergamot, and cinnamon.

## A sensual massage

If you are not used to giving massages, don't worry. You will be amazed at how easy it is to give genuine relief and pleasure. Before you start, place your hands in a basin of hot water to warm them up. Make sure your partner is lying flat and in a comfortable position, and that the room is cozy and warm. Squeeze some oil onto the shoulders and gently massage it into the skin. Let your fingers follow the body's contours, gliding and caressing, enjoying the sensation in your fingertips, and using your loving touch. Work your way over the whole body, from fingertips to toes, skirting the most erogenous zones and saving them for last. At this point, the blissful recipient may be rolled over and the massage continued. At this stage, the emphasis may shift from relaxing to arousing. Indeed, you may well find that you fail to complete the massage before things get out of hand. It can, however, be a tantalizing exercise in control to insist that every inch of the body be covered before you get to the point.

*chapter four*

# LOVE PHILTERS

Love philters are the secret potions that seduce and arouse. Their power is derived from the active principles of nature's aphrodisiacs. These are typically extracted and concentrated using spirit-alcohol, which allows our bodies to absorb them more quickly. In the proper dosage, alcohol can release inhibitions and anxieties, and increase sensitivity and attraction. It also helps us concoct the greatest love potions of them all.

# African Queen

*From Africa, a luscious
liqueur to stimulate and arouse*

## You will need

1 tbsp (15ml) vodka

2 tbsp (30ml)
Cointreau

6 tbsp (90ml)
Amarula Cream

ice cubes

vanilla ice cream
(optional)

blender

On the plains of Africa grows an uncultivated tree. Its scientific name is *sclerocarya birrea*, but it is more commonly known as the marula tree. At the height of the African summer, the olive green, plum-sized fruit of the tree ripens to a golden yellow, and its tropical fragrance floats on the warm summer breeze, luring various species of wild animals from miles around. In particular, herds of trumpeting elephant walk for days to gorge themselves on the fruit, and for this reason the marula tree has come to be known as "the elephant tree." The female tree bears the exotic-tasting fruit, which contains four times as much vitamin C as an average orange. Held to have strong aphrodisiac properties, the marula tree features prominently in many tribal fertility rites. In ancient folklore it was known as "the marriage tree" and even today many rural people conduct wedding ceremonies under its fertile branches. A superb cream liqueur is made from this mystical tree: Amarula Cream. Amarula Cream is rich, soft, and delicious, and is widely available. Straight up, or on the rocks, it makes an excellent cocktail.

## Method

Combine the vodka, Cointreau, Amarula Cream and two or three ice cubes in a blender. Blend until smooth. Pour into a glass and garnish with grated nutmeg. You can also make this drink into a delicious milkshake by adding a few scoops of vanilla ice cream.

# CARIBBEAN CRUISE

*An exotic love juice from
the sunny Caribbean islands*

## YOU WILL NEED

25 fl oz (70cl) bottle
of dark Caribbean
rum

*bois bandé bark*

*mango juice*

*lime juice*

Bois bandé, French for "erect wood," is the local name for a species of Caribbean tree (*Richeria garndis*) that is famous in the islands for its aphrodisiac properties. The bark is torn off in strips and macerated in rum, or dried for use in infusions. Several commercial rums are made with bois bandé, but it is more fun, more potent, and probably cheaper to make your own bois bandé rum. At this point it must be said that there are no clinical reports on the effectiveness or toxicity of bois bandé, but it is safe to say that any ill effects would be well established in folklore by now—it has, after all, been used in the islands for centuries. The following recipe is pretty standard, and the inclusion of mango juice is not just to make it more delicious. Mangoes are considered by many to be highly erotic in their own right, and the use of mango oil as a love potion is quite well established.

## METHOD

Pour off 4 tbsp (60ml) of rum from the bottle and fill it back to the top with pieces of bois bandé bark. Replace the cap and place the bottle in a warm, dark place for at least three weeks. Mix with fresh mango juice and a squeeze of lime for an exotic island love juice.

# Green Goddess

*The ingredients of this amorous libation
have been kept secret for centuries*

## You will need

*1 tbsp (15ml)
Green Chartreuse
per champagne flute*

*champagne*

*champagne flutes*

Herbal liqueurs have been made for centuries, and were originally medicinal cordials infused with the virtues of many different plants. The greatest liqueurs in the world are the various types of Chartreuse. In the 17th century, the Maréchal d'Estrées gave the Monastery of the Grand Chartreuse an already ancient manuscript containing the secret formula of an elixir bestowing long life. The monks provided the elixir to the local people as a medicine, but its fame soon spread far and wide, so they adapted the recipe, adding honey to make a more palatable cordial for daily drinking. Thus was Green Chartreuse born in 1745, and it is still made in the same way today. As for how it is made, all we know is that the complex formula lists 130 ingredients, nearly all herbal, advising where and when the herbs should be picked. We are unlikely to find out more about the recipe, as it is known by only three monks. We do know that there are no artificial ingredients, and that it has an alcohol content of fifty-five percent. Mysterious, intoxicating, and delicious, this potion has gained a reputation for its subtly stimulating and—in the right company—unmistakably arousing effect. This quality is greatly enhanced when mixed with the world's favorite aphrodisiac: champagne.

## Method

Pour the Green Chartreuse into a champagne flute. Top off with chilled champagne and prepare to be enraptured.

Sealed potion ☞

# Love Potion number 9

*A powerful love philter that draws*
*upon the amorous energies of Venus*

## You will need

½ oz (15g) damiana

¼ oz (7g) muira
puama

½ oz (15g) saw
palmetto berries

½ oz (15g) coriander
seeds

1 tbsp (15ml)
strawberry vinegar

4 fl oz (100ml)
high-proof alcohol

1 oz (30g) raw honey

cinnamon essence

vanilla essence

mortar and pestle

glass jar and funnel

coffee filter papers

dark glass bottle

This potent love potion combines nine ingredients, including three of the most powerful herbal aphrodisiacs known: damiana, yohimbe, and saw palmetto. The philter should be prepared, at each stage, on a Friday, the day of Venus, to benefit from the energies of this planet of love. The ideal time to prepare it is when the sun is in Taurus, as this sign is ruled by Venus, and spring is traditionally the time of fertility rites and rising sexual energy.

## Method

At sunrise on the first Friday following a new moon, grind to a powder the dry damiana, muira puama, saw palmetto berries, and coriander seeds. Place the powdered herbs in a glass jar. Mix the strawberry vinegar with the alcohol. Pour carefully over the powdered herbs; add more alcohol, if necessary, to cover the herbs. Seal the jar and leave undisturbed in a warm, dark place. At sunrise on the Friday two weeks following, filter the mixture through a glass funnel lined with a paper coffee filter. Press the residue in the filter paper with the back of a wooden spoon to get the last few drops. Pour the raw honey in a cup and warm it by placing the cup in a pan of hot water.

Add the honey to the filtered tincture, together with cinnamon and vanilla essence to taste. Decant into a dark glass bottle. Take 3 tsp (15ml) in a glass of warm water. To achieve a more gradual increase of libido, take seven drops in water twice a day, during the waxing moon, for three months.

# jungle Love juice

*A tantalizing libation
to stimulate desire*

## You will need

*passion fruit juice*

*½ oz (15g) catuaba*

*½ oz (15g) muira
puama*

*½ oz (15g) guarana*

*25 fl oz (70cl) bottle
of white rum*

The Tupi Indians of the Brazilian rainforest praise one plant above all others for its ability to restore or sustain desire: catuaba. So effective is catuaba in maintaining sexual vigor in men that the Indians say "Until a father reaches sixty, the child is his; after that, the child is catuaba's." Catuaba is also a healer and a powerful protector against disease, having antibacterial and antiviral properties. But above all, it is a love tonic. Another famous Amazonian herb, muira puama—a love tonic as well—works very well in synergy with catuaba. Muira puama has many notable medicinal qualities, but is most widely used for impotence, infertility, and menstrual disorders. Many clinical trials have been conducted which support muira puama's reputation. It needs to be carefully processed, however, to release all of its essential properties. The libido-enhancing properties of both muira puama and catuaba are intensified when taken with guarana, another Amazonian wonder plant. Guarana enhances mental alertness and stimulates desire. Brewed together, these plants deliver a potent love tonic.

## Method

Place the catuaba, muira puama, and guarana in a pan with a close-fitting lid. Pour in half of the white rum, cover, and slowly bring to just below boiling point. Allow to infuse for twenty minutes without boiling. Strain back into the half-full rum bottle. Mix with passion fruit juice to taste and have a good time.

# STAG KNIGHT

*A powerful energy tonic that will
increase your libidinous desires*

## YOU WILL NEED

*1 oz (30g)
American ginseng,
powdered*

*1 oz (30g) red deer
antler, powdered*

*grape brandy*

*glass jar*

*dark glass bottle*

The Chinese have always valued parts of certain animals as potent remedies. Unfortunately, the demand for some animal medicines, particularly reputed aphrodisiacs, has led to certain species, such as tigers and rhinoceros, being threatened with extinction in spite of all efforts to prevent poaching. One important animal-derived medicine that does not pose an ecological problem is deer antler. Deer grow a new set of antlers every year, and great numbers are bred in many countries, particularly New Zealand, to supply the demand. Deer antler is a powerful yang (male energy) tonic. It treats impotence, frigidity, infertility, premature ejaculation, and hormonal deficiency in both men and women. One of the most powerful energy tonics, and a potent libido-booster, combines red deer antler with American ginseng. The ginseng balances and complements the effects of the antler.

## METHOD

Place the American ginseng and red deer antler in a glass jar and pour on twice the amount of brandy needed to cover the powder. Seal, and store in a warm, dark place for two weeks. Strain into a dark glass bottle. The liquid can be taken as a general libido tonic, ½ tsp (3ml) twice a day during the waxing moon only; or, occasionally, as a love philter, 2 tbsp (30ml) straight or mixed with water.

# Horny Goat Wine

*A tonic to whet
your appetite for love*

## You will need

*2½ oz (70g) horny
goat weed*

*1½ oz (40g) saw
palmetto or dong
quai*

*1½ oz (40g) yohimbe*

*1½ oz (40g) damiana*

*1½ oz (40g) Chinese
ginseng, powdered*

*1 oz (30g) licorice
root, shredded*

*6 pints (3½L) water*

*3 lb (1.4kg) honey*

*1 tsp (5ml) wine
yeast*

*1 gallon (5L) glass
demijohn, cork, and
airlock*

*wine bottles, corks*

The potent aphrodisiac qualities of horny goat weed (*epimedium sagittatum*), damiana (*turnera aphrodisiaca*), and yohimbe (*corynanthe yohimbé*) are discussed in the Aphrodite's Secrets chapter. Here they are combined to powerful effect in this ancient Chinese recipe for a tonic wine, which is especially suitable for women. The same recipe can be used for men, substituting saw palmetto for dong quai. The process is best begun at sunrise on the first Friday following a new moon.

## Method

Take the horny goat weed, saw palmetto or dong quai, yohimbe, damiana, Chinese ginseng, and licorice root and place in a large pan with the water. Cover the pan, bring to a boil, and simmer gently for fifteen minutes. Allow to cool for ten minutes, then add the raw honey. Stir until the honey is dissolved. Allow to cool to room temperature, approximately 65–75°F (18–24°C), and add wine yeast. Cover with a cloth and allow to ferment for a few days, then siphon into a glass demijohn and fit with cork and airlock. Once the brew has stopped fizzing, fermentation is complete. Strain and filter into wine bottles that have been washed and boiled in water for five minutes, then cork. The wine should keep for about a year, but the sooner it is consumed, the better. As a tonic, drink half a glass three times a day. On nights of passion you can be more indulgent, but be warned: this is a potent brew.

# Joy Stick

*This sexy concoction will go
straight to your erogenous zone*

## You will need

*celery juice*

*tomato juice*

*Worcester sauce*

*fino sherry*

*orange juice*

*celery salt*

*white pepper*

*salt*

*Tabasco sauce*

*vodka*

*celery stalks*

In Europe, celery has long been celebrated as an aphrodisiac. Until recently, however, science assumed that celery's long-standing reputation as a libido booster owed more to its vaguely phallic shape than to any real aphrodisiac qualities, but it now seems that the ancients had it right all along. Celery stimulates the pituitary gland, which helps release sexual hormones in the body. It also contains complex oils which may have a stimulating effect on the olfactory and sexual centers in the brain. There are even reports that it contains small amounts of methaqualone, the notorious "love drug" that was popular in the United States during the 1970s (under the name of Quaalude). If celery really does contain this substance, you can be sure that the amount will be minimal, but it adds further fuel to celery's sexy reputation. Tomatoes, too, are considered by some to have arousing qualities, which may explain why they used to be called "love apples." Celery and tomato juice combine perfectly to make a Bloody Mary with a difference.

## Method

Combine equal measures of celery juice and tomato juice in a jug with a few shakes of Worcester sauce, a splash of fino sherry, a splash of orange juice, a shake of celery salt, and white pepper, salt, and Tabasco sauce to taste. Pour into tall glasses over vodka and ice and garnish with a celery stalk.

# EL JEQUE

*A sexy Mexican treat that will*
*raise the temperature of your passion*

## YOU WILL NEED

*bottle of Californian*
*red wine*

*1 oz (30g) damiana*
*leaves*

*2–3 dried red chili*
*peppers*

Mexico is home to some of the world's greatest aphrodisiacs and love foods. The Aztecs and other native groups used a number of local herbs to revive and sustain flagging libidos, as well as plenty of chili peppers to spice up their cooking. Chilies cause the body to release feel-good chemicals into the system, so if you can take the heat, make out in the kitchen! The ancient Mexicans used many other powerful plants for sacred and amorous pursuits, but most of them are now illegal or too dangerous to recommend. Nowadays, most Mexicans content themselves with a dazzling array of local brews made from an astonishing variety of fruits and plants, such as the spiky agaves, from which they make pulque, mescal, and tequila. In Oaxaca, they add the "worm" that feeds off the agave to the mescal, believing it to have libidinous qualities. But the most popular aphrodisiac in the land, and famous now around the world, is damiana (*turnera aphrodisiaca*), due to its surefire reputation. Here is a way to imbibe this wonderful herb in a delicious drink. It is called "el jeque," which is Spanish for "the sheik."

## METHOD

Pour yourself half a glass of Californian red wine—merlot or shiraz, for example (make sure the bottle has a cork). Fill the bottle back up with the damiana leaf and a couple of dried red chili peppers. Cork tightly and leave in a warm place for a week. Filter and enjoy a glass with a very close friend.

# BELLA MARGARITA

*A lascivious cocktail guaranteed
to quench your thirst for love*

## YOU WILL NEED

*silver tequila*

*lime juice*

*triple sec orange
liqueur*

*crema de damiana*

*ice*

*salt*

Cocktails were first drunk in the United States during Prohibition and caught on in a big way. They represent glamor, sophistication, permissiveness, and pleasure. As tools of mutual seduction, they are unrivaled. One of the world's greatest cocktails is the margarita. No one knows for sure how it got its name, but we know that it first appeared in Mexico City and Acapulco in the 1940s. The recipe is known all over the world, the ingredients being tequila, lime juice, and triple sec, but some authorities insist that the first margaritas were made with damiana liqueur rather than triple sec—damiana *(turnera aphrodisiaca)* being Mexico's favorite aphrodisiac plant. Track down a bottle of crema de damiana (or make it yourself using the recipe on page 116) and you will have the secret ingredient to make one of the world's greatest love philters. Do not be tempted to blend it with crushed ice—this is no slush puppy.

## METHOD

For the best margarita in town, mix three parts silver tequila, three parts lime juice, and one part triple sec orange liqueur (Cointreau is the best) with one part crema de damiana. Shake with ice and strain into chilled, salt-rimmed glasses. Try not to drink too many before getting to the point.

# CREMA DE DAMIANA

*The secret weapon of Mexican
lovers since ancient times*

## You will need

*1 oz (30g) damiana
leaves*

*2 cups (500ml)
aguardiente or
tequila*

*8 fl oz (200ml)
spring water*

*1 lb (450g) raw
honey*

*glass jar*

*glass bottle*

Damiana (*turnera aphrodisiaca*), along with chocolate, has been Mexico's favorite aphrodisiac since the time of the Aztecs. This attractive little shrub grows wild throughout Mexico. Now that it is used medicinally all over the world, it is commercially cultivated on a large scale. There are many ways of taking damiana, the most fun being with alcohol. There is a delicious liqueur called crema de damiana (also called licore de damiana) which is sold commercially in bottles shaped like the torso of a pregnant woman—actually a pre-Columbian fertility goddess, possibly Mayahuel, the highly erotic Aztec goddess of aphrodisiac plants and inebriation. A bottle of crema de damiana is traditionally given as a honeymoon present to newlyweds on account of its encouraging effects. Here's how to make your own.

## METHOD

Put the damiana leaves in a glass jar and cover with the aguardiente (Mexican cane liquor) or tequila. Seal the jar and leave in a warm, dark place for ten days. Strain into a bottle and return the leaves to the jar. Cover with the spring water and leave for two days. Strain into a pan and heat gently. Dissolve the raw honey in the water. Let the water cool and add it to the bottle with the alcohol extract. This philter improves with age, so leave it for at least a month, during which time it will become crystal clear. Decant and strain off the sediment. Drink straight up or on the rocks.

# KAVA KAVA

*A gentle tonic that captures the*
*magic of the Polynesian islands*

## YOU WILL NEED

1 oz (30g) kava kava
root, powdered

2 cups (500ml) milk
(preferably goat's)

lemongrass

fresh ginger root

honey

When Captain Cook first arrived in the Polynesian islands,
he and his men could not believe how open and innocent the
beautiful islanders were, particularly in matters of love. The
men were immediately captivated by the island women—
indeed, so intoxicated were they that they found it very hard
to leave, even on pain of death. One of the secrets of the
islanders was a very special brew called kava kava. This was
the hub of social and cultural life, and a drink of sacred
significance. It was, and still is, prepared from the huge roots
of the kava kava shrub. The drinking of kava promotes a
tranquil and friendly state of well-being, which allows deep,
dreamless sleep with no hangover. No wonder it is acquiring
a growing reputation in the West as a brew to be shared by
lovers who value its calming, gently stimulating properties.

## METHOD

Whisk the kava kava root into the milk. Add a stick of
lemongrass and a couple of fine slices of fresh ginger root. Warm
gently and allow to infuse for ten minutes, stirring occasionally.
Do not allow to boil. Sweeten with honey to taste and prepare
to engage with your lover sooner rather than later.

The sexiest philter

# ABSINTHE: THE GREEN

Absinthe has a legendary reputation as a dangerously debilitating spirit, and was beloved by bohemian writers and artists in 19th-century Europe. By World War I, it had been banned in many European countries.

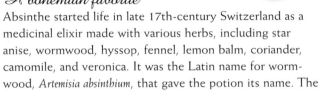

# FAIRY

## A bohemian favorite

Absinthe started life in late 17th-century Switzerland as a medicinal elixir made with various herbs, including star anise, wormwood, hyssop, fennel, lemon balm, coriander, camomile, and veronica. It was the Latin name for wormwood, *Artemisia absinthium*, that gave the potion its name. The drink soon became popular as an aperitif and, by the 1850s, the French were drinking more absinthe than cognac. Around that time it became associated with radical bohemian artists such as Baudelaire and Rimbaud, who were scandalizing polite society with their experimentation with opium and hashish. The bohemians wrote paeons in praise of absinthe as a creative muse and liberator.

## Debilitating or liberating?

Although beloved by some, others took the view that absinthe was an evil drug, and soon it became linked with degeneracy. Its primary problem was that it was cheap and very strong—around 70 percent alcohol. Also, it contains a compound which stimulates the central nervous system, and can, if chronically abused, damage it. Taken in moderation, however, absinthe is a wonderful potion, promoting intimacy and a liberated imagination, while its wicked past lends an exciting edge.

## A safe and delicious variant

Absinthe is banned in the US and some other countries, but you can make a similar variant yourself. Simply put ½ oz (15g) each of fennel seeds, aniseed, hyssop, lemon balm, and damiana in a quart (1L) jar, along with ¼ oz (7g) of wormwood. Cover with a 700ml bottle of vodka. Seal and store in a warm, dark place for two weeks, shaking occasionally, then strain and bottle. Drink with ice and water and indulge in some Old European romance.

# DIRECTORY

Absinthe A strongly alcoholic aniseed-flavored herbal liquor containing wormwood. Banned in the US and several other countries.

Aguardiente A clear Mexican spirit distilled from sugar cane. Available commercially.

Anemone (*Anemone spp.*) A genus of flowering plants in the buttercup family.

Anise/aniseed (*Pimpinella anisum*) The aromatic seeds of a Middle Eastern plant.

Bayleaf (*Laurus nobilis*) The leaf of the bay laurel tree, commonly used as a culinary herb.

Bergamot (*Citrus bergamia*) A variety of orange. An essential oil is derived from its rind.

Bois bandé (*Roupala montana*) A species of Caribbean gommai tree.

Broom (*Cytisus scoparius*) A tall flowering shrub. Used medicinally for heart conditions.

Caraway (*Carum carvi*) A member of the umbellifer family. Cultivated for its spicy, aromatic seeds.

Cardamom (*Elettaria cardamomum*) The pods of this plant are prized as a delicate, aromatic spice.

Catuaba (*Anemopaegma mirandum*) An Amazonian herb used as an aphrodisiac.

Chaste tree (*Vitex agnus-castus*) The seeds of this shrub can be used to regulate hormones.

Chypre A generic name for an exotic type of perfume. Originally made from a variety of ingredients from Cyprus.

Cilantro See coriander, below.

Citric acid A natural acid derived from citrus fruits. Sold in powdered crystal form.

Civet A member of the cat family. The male produces a musky substance that is an ingredient in many perfumes.

Clary sage (*Salvia sclarea*) A member of the sage family. The essential oil is used in perfumes as a fixative or musk substitute.

Cloves (*Eugenia caryophylus*) The dried flower buds of the clove tree. Powerful and pungent, they are used as a spice.

Coca (*Erythoxylum coca*) An evergreen shrub of the South American Andes that has been used medicinally for many centuries.

Columbine (*Aquilegia vulgaris*) A European wildflower, now a popular garden plant.

Copal (*Copaifera lansdorfii*) The resin of a South American species of the copaiba tree. Used as a ceremonial incense in Latin America.

Coriander (*Coriandrum sativum*) Also known as cilantro. A member of the umbellifer family, the seeds are used as a spice.

Cornflower (*Centaurea cyanus/montana*) Two separate but similar species of European wildflower. Both are used as love charms.

Cowslip (*Primula veris*) A European wildflower, similar to primrose.

Cubeb (*Piper cubeba*) A hot, spicy type of peppercorn, often used in Indonesian cooking.

Cumin (*Cuminum cyminum*) A member of the umbellifer family and a relative of coriander (cilantro) and caraway.

**Damiana** (*Turnera diffusa, aphrodisiaca*) A shrub found in Mexico and the southern US.

**Dong quai** (*Angelica sinensis*) Also spelled "dang gui," and otherwise known as Chinese angelica, this is an important women's herb.

**Evening primrose** (*Oenothera biennis*) A European flower. The oil derived from its seeds is used to treat skin problems.

**Fennel** (*Foeniculum vugare*) A member of the umbellifer family. The bulb is eaten as a vegetable, while the seeds are used as a spice.

**Flax** (*Linum usitatissimum*) A medium-sized herb with a pretty blue flower. Grown commercially as the source of linen and linseed.

**Frankincense** (*Boswellia sacra*) An aromatic resin exuded in pear-shaped droplets by a small tree native to Arabia. Also known as olibanum.

**Galbanum** (*Ferula galbaniflua, syn. gummosa*) A small perennial herb native to northern Asia Minor. Its resin is used in perfumes.

**Ginseng, American** (*Panax quinquefolium*) A close relative of Chinese ginseng, but this version is considered slightly milder.

**Ginseng, Chinese** (*Panax ginseng*) The "original" ginseng, the root of which is highly prized in China as a panacea (cure-all) and mild stimulant.

**Grains of Paradise** (*Aframomum melegueta*) An aromatic spice used both in African and Caribbean cooking and as an aphrodisiac.

**Green Chartreuse** A classic herbal liqueur that has been made by the Carthusian monks since the 18th century. The recipe is a secret.

**Guarana** (*Paullinia cupana*) An Amazonian plant, the seeds of which can increase sexual desire.

**Heartsease** (*Viola tricolor*) Commonly known as the wild pansy. Used as a love charm.

**Hedge hyssop** (*Gratiola officinalis*) A flowering plant found in Europe that was once used medicinally.

**Herb Paris** (*Paris quadrifolia*) Also known as "true love" and "true love knot." Used as a love charm.

**Horny goat weed** (*Epimedium sagittatum*) A potent plant aphrodisiac from China, where it is called *yin yang huo*.

**Horsetail** (*Equisetum arvense*) Also known as "shave grass," this fern grows throughout the northern hemisphere, and has been used medicinally for centuries.

**Hyssop** (*Hyssopus officinalis*) An ancient medicinal herb that is an ingredient in absinthe and Chartreuse.

**Jasmine** (*Jasminum officinale*) A deciduous climber with scented flowers, which are used in perfume and to flavor tea.

**Kahlua** A fine coffee-based liqueur.

**Kava Kava** (*Piper methysticum*) The roots of this Polynesian shrub are used to make a ceremonial brew with euphoric properties.

**Lady's mantle** (*Alchemilla vulgaris*) Used to tone the female reproductive system.

**Lady's slipper** (*Cypridium parviflorum, var. pubescens*) A pungent member of the orchid family. Also known as American valerian.

**Lavender** (*Lavandula angustifolia*) An aromatic herb, the essential oil of which is used in aromatherapy. It is also antibiotic and insecticidal. The dried flowers are used to flavor tea.

**Lemon balm** (*Melissa officinalis*) A medicinal

# Directory

herb. Useful for calming hyperactive children.

**Lemon grass** *(Cymbopogon citratus)* A bitter, aromatic herb. Commonly used in Thai cooking, and in the West as a tea flavoring.

**Lily** *(Lilium spp.)* A family of flowering plants.

**Love-in-a-mist** *(Nigella damascena)* An attractive flower with blue blossoms, common to parts of Europe and Asia. Its seeds are used medicinally and in cooking.

**Lustral water** Purifying water that was used cermonially by the Druids.

**Mandrake** *(Mandragora officinarum)* A rare and mysterious Old World plant steeped in myth and folklore. Not to be confused with American Mandrake.

**Marshmallow** *(Althea officinalis)* A medicinal herb that is native to Europe and has become naturalized in the US.

**Merlot** A variety of grape that is used to produce a mellow red wine of the same name.

**Monkshood** *(Aconitum napellus)* A garden flower native to Europe. The roots contain a poison called aconite that is used medicinally.

**Motherwort** *(Leonurus cardiaca)* One of the classic women's herbs. Native to Europe, but widely grown in gardens in the US.

**Mugwort** *(Artemisia vulgaris)* A European medicinal herb. Its aromatic leaves are used to purify physical and spiritual spaces.

**Muira Puama** *(Liriosma ovata)* A tree that is native to Brazil.

The root is used as an aphrodisiac and tonic. Also known as potentwood.

**Musk** A substance produced by the Musk deer and some other animals. Highly prized as a perfume. Now produced synthetically.

**Myrrh** *(Commiphora myrrha)* An aromatic resin exuded in drops by a shrub native to Arabia.

**Neroli** *(Citrus aurantium)* An expensive essential oil derived from bitter oranges. Possesses skin-rejuvenating qualities.

**Olibanum** See Frankincense, above.

**Orchid** *(Orchidaceae spp.)* A large family of flowering plants. Some species are considered aphrodisiacs because of the shape of the bulb.

**Orpine** *(Sedum telephium)* A European wildflower found in shady places. Used as a love charm.

**Pasque flower** *(Pulsatilla spp.)* A genus of attractive flowering plants found in Europe.

**Patchouli** *(Pogestemon patchouli)* A fragrant tropical herb. Its essential oil is used in perfume. Uplifting in small doses and sedative in larger ones.

**Periwinkle** *(Vinca minor/major)* A flowering plant common to Europe and the US. Used medicinally and as a love charm.

**Pine nuts** Pine cone seeds that have long been esteemed as an aphrodisiac.

**Potentwood** *(Liriosma ovata)* See Muira puama, above.

**Primrose** *(Primula vulgaris)* A pale yellow spring flower found in Europe.

**Queen's delight** *(Stillingia sylvatica)* Found in North America, the root of this herb is used as a skin tonic.

**Saffron** *(Crocus sativus)* The dried stigmas of this crocus species produce a yellow dye, and are also used as an aphrodisiac, a spice, and medicinally as a blood vitalizer.

Sage *(Salvia officinalis)* A culinary and medicinal herb. The leaves and stems can be dried, burned, and used as incense or an air purifier.

Sandalwood *(Santalum album)* The heartwood of this tropical tree produces a highly prized aromatic oil that is commonly used as incense and in perfumes.

Sarsaparilla *(Smilax officinalis)* A New World plant that is used in native medicine. The root is now used worldwide as a tonic.

Sassafras *(Sassafras albidum)* Thought to be the first medicinal plant to be introduced into Europe from the New World.

Satyrion The most famous aphrodisiac of classical Europe. Now extinct, it was probably a species of orchid.

Saw Palmetto *(Sabal serrulata)* A small palm tree found on the south Atlantic coast of the US. The berries are used as a prostate tonic.

Shiraz A variety of grape which produces a rich, spicy red wine of the same name.

Smudge stick The dried leaves and stems of aromatic herbs such as sage, mugwort, or lavender, tied into tight bundles and burned as incense or an air purifier.

Summer savory *(Satureja hortensis)* A culinary herb with an aphrodisiacal reputation.

Toadflax *(Linaria vulgaris)* A short-to-medium yellow flowering European herb.

Tobacco *(Nicotiana tabacum)* Many varieties of this plant genus have beautiful flowers.

Vervain *(Verbena officinalis)* A medicinal herb native to the US and Europe. Most potent when just flowering. Used as a love charm.

Violet *(Viola odorata)* A delicate, sweet-smelling European spring flower. Used as a love charm.

Wheatgerm oil A rich oil derived from wheat kernels. High in vitamin E, it is used as an antioxidant.

Wild oats *(Avena sativa)* The unripe (green), milky seeds of this cereal grass are a valuable libido tonic.

Wormwood *(Artemisia absinthium)* Aromatic and very bitter, this medicinal herb is a principle ingredient in absinthe.

Yarrow *(Achillea millefolium)* A wildflower common to the US and Europe. Valued for its medicinal and divinatory properties.

Yeast A fungus used to leaven bread and ferment sugar to form alcohol.

Ylang Ylang *(Cananga odorata)* An essential oil is produced from the flowers of this tropical tree. Often used in perfume.

Yohimbe *(Pausinystalia yohimbe, syn. Corynanthe yohimbe)* The bark of this tender evergreen West African tree is used as an aphrodisiac. It is the only plant that is officially accepted by orthodox pharmacologists as an aphrodisiac.

Yohimbine A drug derived from Yohimbe (see above), with proven aphrodisiac qualities. Sold commercially.

# Buyers' Guide

## UK

G. Baldwin & Co.,
173 Walworth Road,
London SE17 1RW
Tel: (020) 7703 5550
Website: www.baldwins.co.uk

Gnostic Garden
P.O. Box 242
Newcastle upon Tyne, NE99 1ED
Website: www.gnosticgarden.co.uk

Neal's Yard Remedies
Neal's Yard, Covent Garden
London WC2H 9DP
Tel: (020) 7379 0705
Website: www.nealsyardremedies.com

Wildweed
Witherdon Manor
Beaworthy, Devon
EX21 5BS.
Tel: (0183) 787 1571

## USA & CANADA

Aphrodisia Products Inc.
62 Kent St
Brooklyn, NY 11222
Tel: 1-800-221-6898
Website: www.aphrodisiaproducts.com

Companion Plants
7247 N. Coolville Ridge Rd.
Athens, Ohio 4570
Tel: (740) 593-3092
Website: www.companionplants.com

Dances with Herbs
P.O. Box 1100
Idyllwild, CA 92549
Tel: (909) 659-5545

Good Medicine Cabin
P.O. Box 138
Bartonsville PA 183211
Tel:1-800-606-3248
Website: www.goodmedicinecabin.com

Herb Market
P.O. Box 2127
Elk Grove, CA 95759
Tel: (916) 686-2555
Website: www.herbmarket.com

Leaves And Roots
9434 E. Colonial Drive
Orlando, FLA 32817
Tel: (407) 823-8840
Website: www.leavesandroots.com

Stony Mountain Botanicals Ltd.
155 N Water St.
Loudonville, OH 44842
Tel: (419) 994-4857

# Index